ndala is a Sanskrit word which means "circle" or "discoid
ect" is a geometric design holding significance in many cul
Buddhism and Hinduism.
ndalas are symbolic of different aspects of the universe. It
instrumental to meditation and symbolizes prayer in diffe
ts of the world, especially, Tibet, China and Japan.

ave recently gained a lot of reputation in the world of art
rapy and as a means to alleviate symptoms of stress, anxie
ression and several other mental health issues.

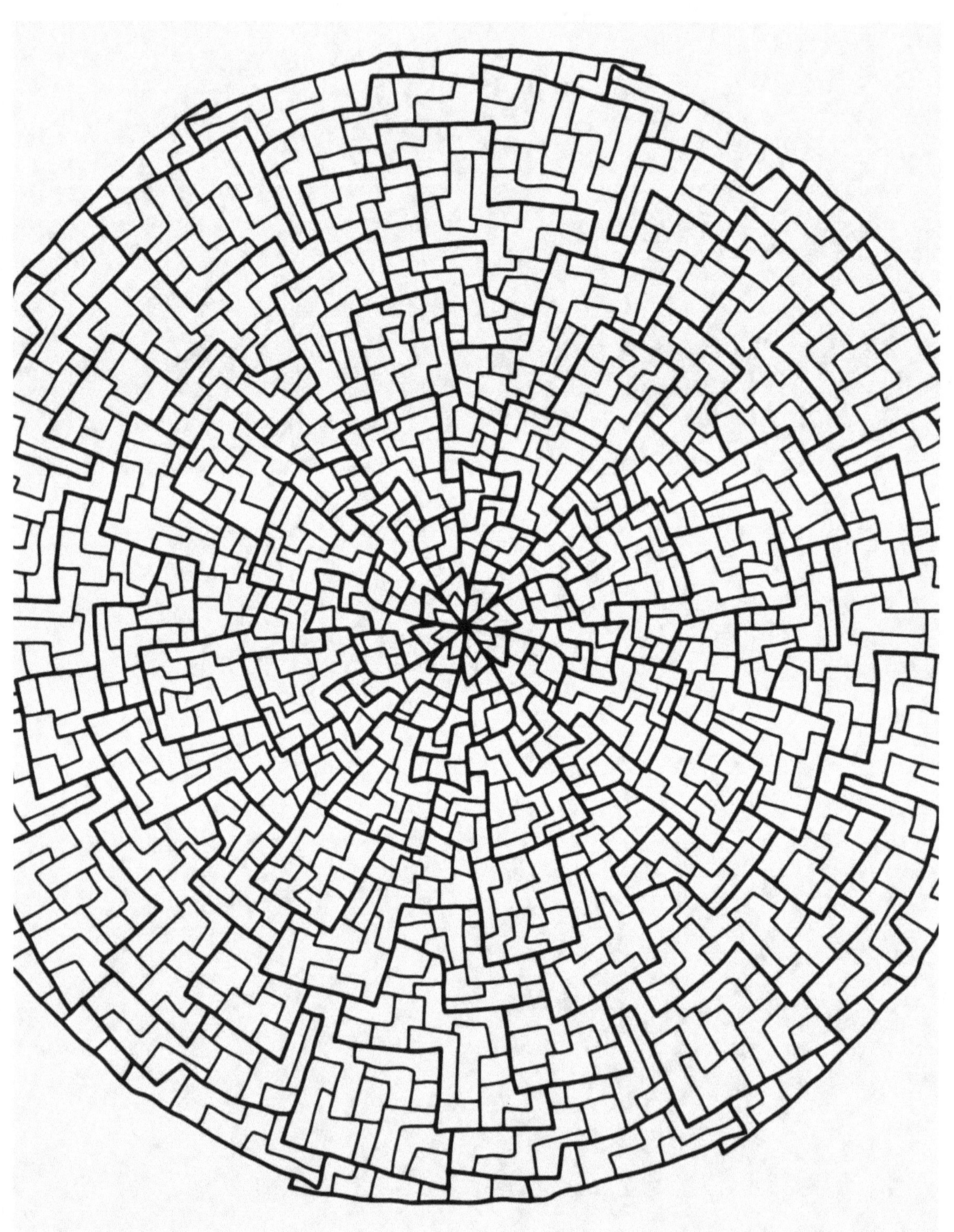

Thank you
for your
purchase